Once upon a time, there was a little girl named Imaan. She loved going to bed every night because she would always have the most amazing dreams.

One night, as she drifted off to sleep, she found herself soaring through the vast expanse of space.

Sun

The Sun was shining bright and warm in Imaan's dream. It was the center of our solar system, providing light and heat to all the planets.

Imaan felt its warmth on her face as she gazed at the star. She learned that the Sun is so massive that it makes up over 99% of the total mass of our solar system. She was amazed by its power and beauty.

Moon

As Imaan continued her journey, she saw the Moon, glowing in the night sky.

It was a beautiful ball of light, reflecting the light of the sun. She learned that the moon is Earth's only natural satellite and helps regulate our planet's tides. Imaan was fascinated by the way the moon changed shape throughout the month, from a tiny sliver to a full, round disk.

Next, Imaan saw Mercury, the smallest planet in our solar system.

Despite its size, it had a big personality, with a surface covered in craters and rocks. Imaan learned that Mercury is the closest planet to the sun and experiences extreme temperature changes. She was amazed that such a small planet could have such a unique surface and environment.

Venus

As Imaan continued her journey, she came across Venus, the second planet from the sun.

Venus was known for its brightness and beauty and Imaan could see why. The planet was covered in a thick atmosphere that reflected the sun's light and made it shine even brighter. Imaan learned that Venus has a toxic atmosphere and a surface temperature hot enough to melt lead.

Next, Imaan saw Earth, her home planet, and was filled with wonder and pride.

She saw the blue oceans, green forests, and white clouds from space. Imaan learned that Earth is the only known planet with liquid water and is home to over 7 billion people and countless species of plants and animals. She felt grateful to live on such a beautiful and diverse planet.

Mars

Imaan saw a red planet Mars as she kept exploring.

People call it the red planet because it is red from iron, which looks like rust. Mars has a huge volcano and a deep canyon.

Imaan was amazed by how different Mars looked and wanted to explore it.

Imaan saw the biggest planet next!

It was Jupiter, a giant gas planet with dark clouds and big storms. Jupiter has 79 moons and a giant red spot that has been storming for hundreds of years! Imaan was so shocked by how huge and strong Jupiter was!

Saturn

Imaan saw a magical planet with shiny rings! The rings were made of ice, rocks, and dust that sparkled.

Saturn is the second biggest planet and has lots of moons! Imaan was so excited to see the pretty rings around Saturn! She couldn't believe how beautiful it was!

Imaan saw a blue planet far away next.

Uranus was special because it spun on its side, with its poles facing the sun. Uranus is called an ice giant and has 13 rings. Uranus also has 27 moons and a ring system around it. Imaan was surprised by how Uranus spun in a strange way.

Imaan saw a blue planet far away in space. Neptune was like Uranus, but even further from the sun.

Neptune has short days, long years and is an ice giant, gassy planet with moons and faint rings. Imaan learned that Neptune also has 14 moons and winds that blow very fast. She was amazed by the beauty and mystery of this distant world.

Finally, Imaan saw Pluto, a small, icy world at the edge of the solar system.

Despite its small size, Pluto had a big personality and was once considered the ninth planet. Imaan learned that Pluto was now classified as a dwarf planet and had five moons of its own. She was fascinated by the smallest and most distant planet in our solar system and the mysteries it held.

Imaan woke up with her heart racing with excitement.

She had just dreamed of traveling through the solar system and seeing all eight planets, the Sun, and even the distant, extinct planet of Pluto. She knew that her dream was a sign that she was destined for a new adventure and she couldn't wait to see where it would take her.

www.ingramcontent.com/pod-product-compliance
Lightning Source LLC
Chambersburg PA
CBHW041126130526
44590CB00054B/78